KISS MY ASS SERIES

Amusing Swear Words To Color

For Stress Releasing

By

Queenie McJody

Happy Coloring!

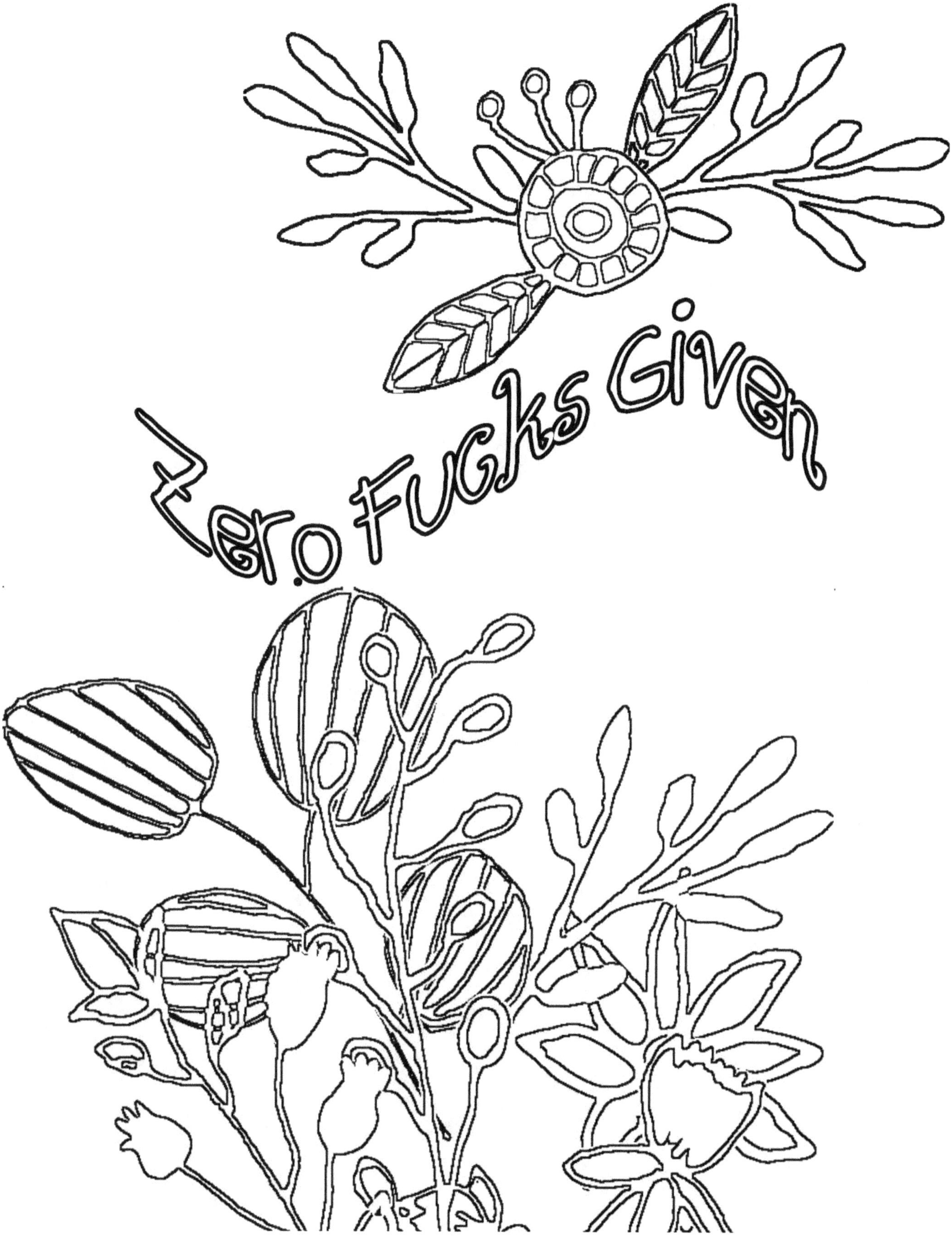
Zero Fucks Given

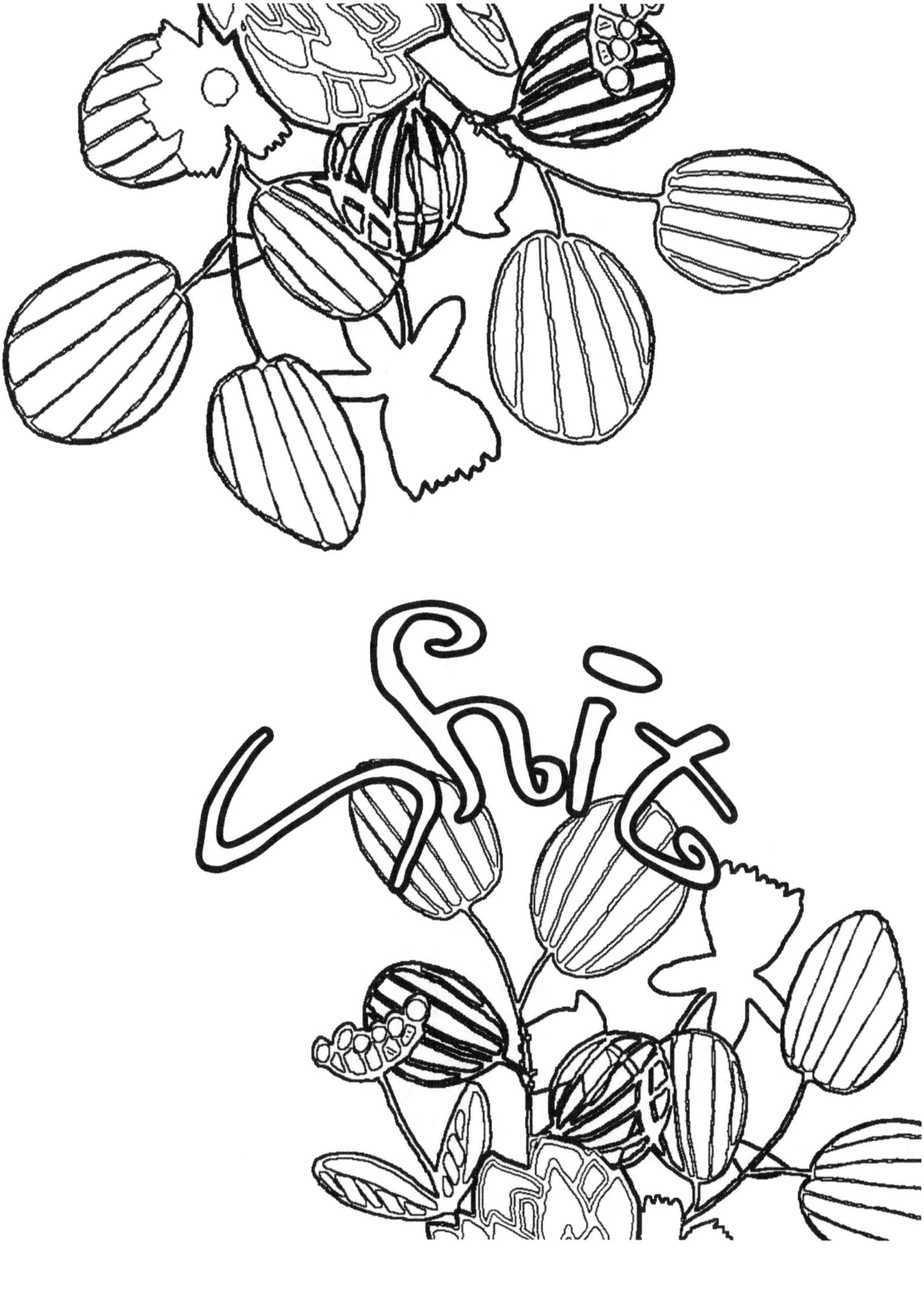
Shit

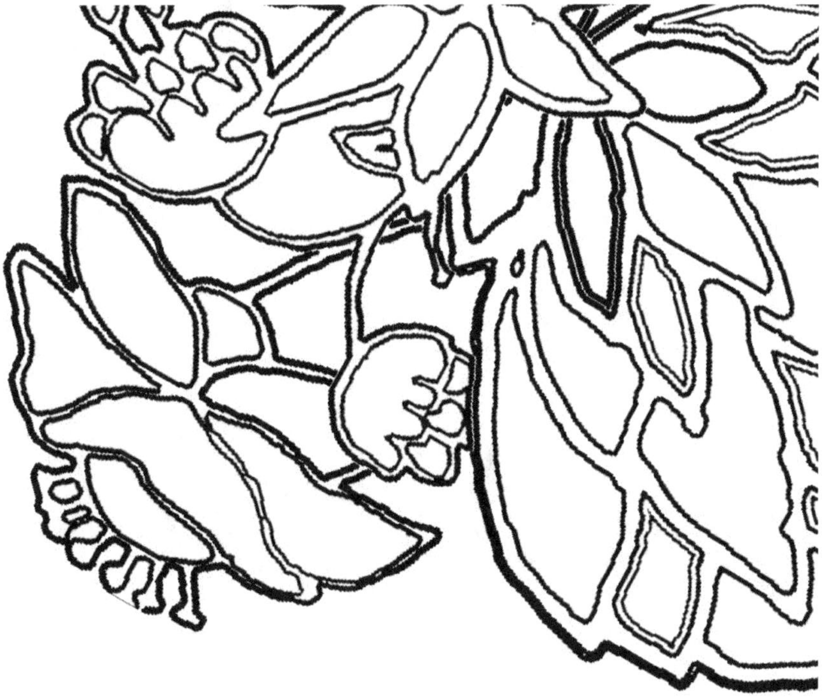

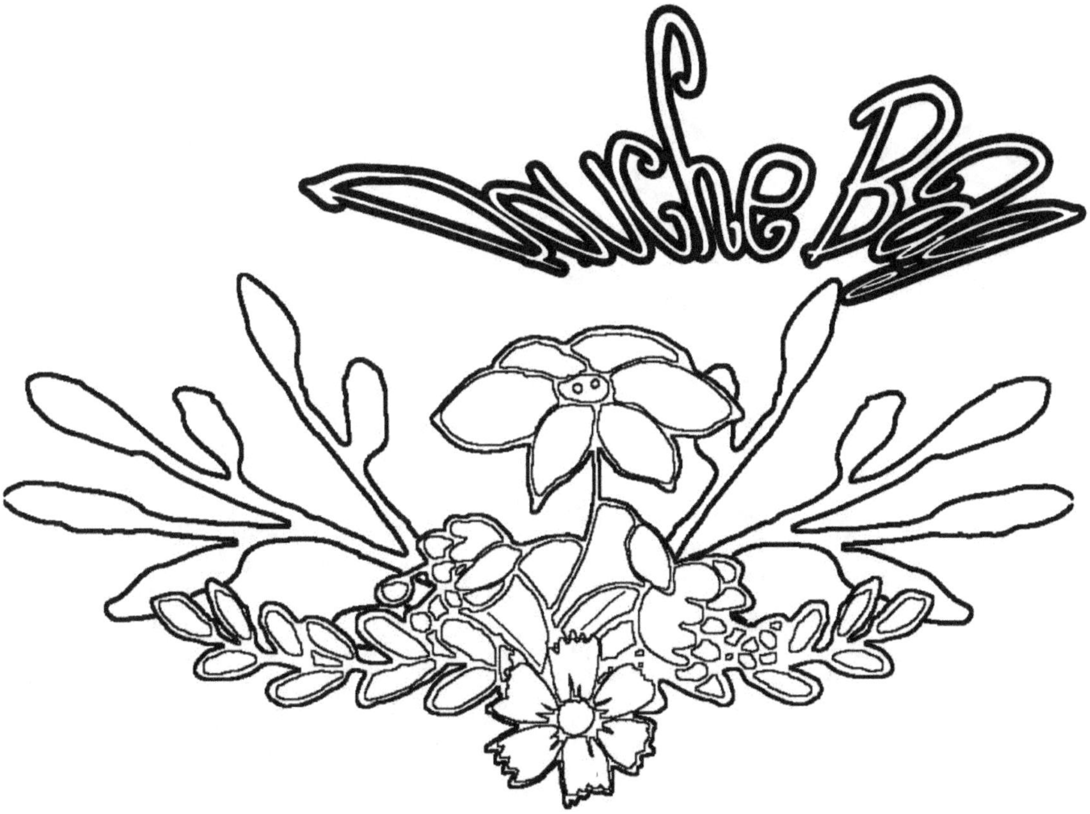
Douche Bag

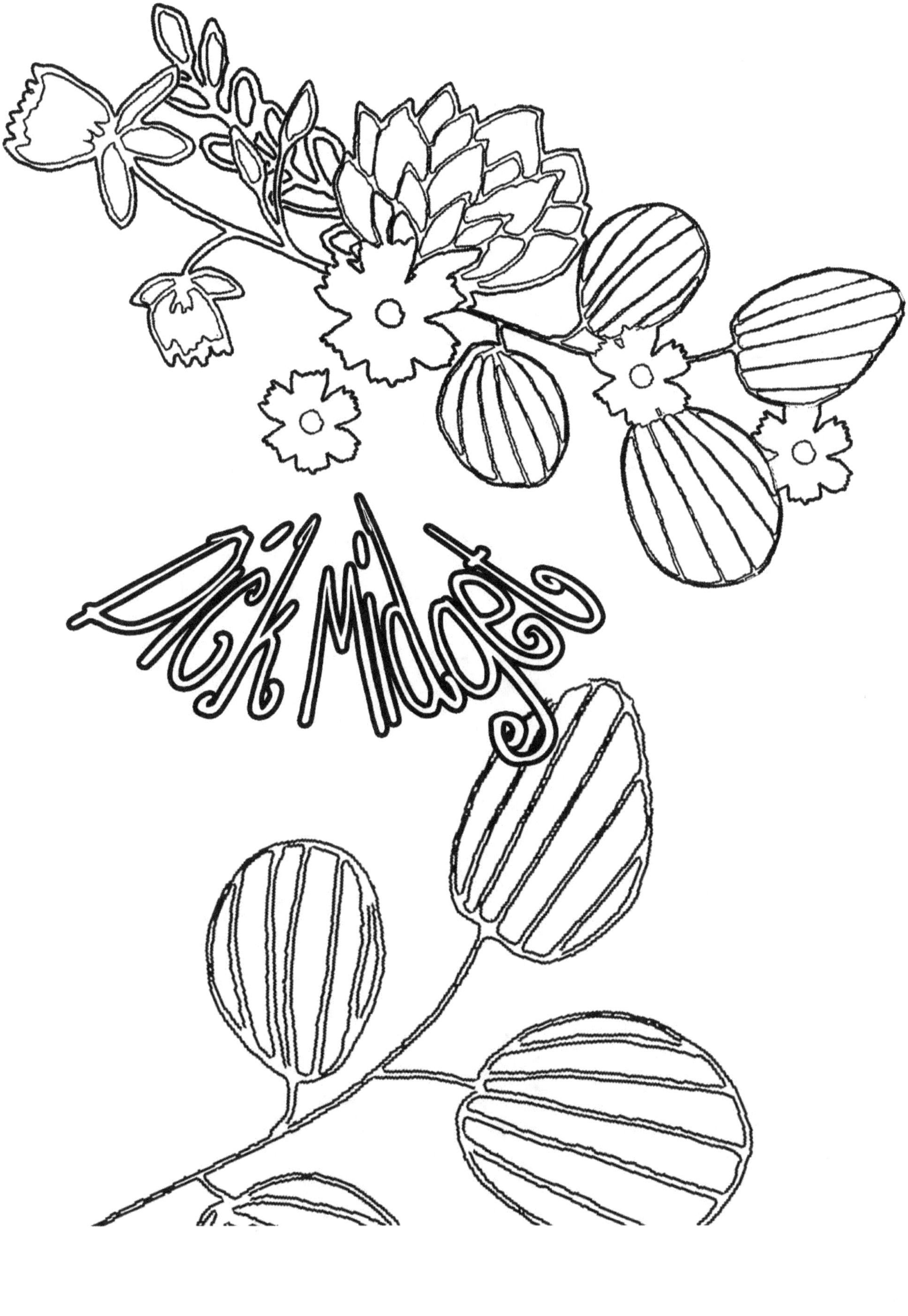
Dick Midget

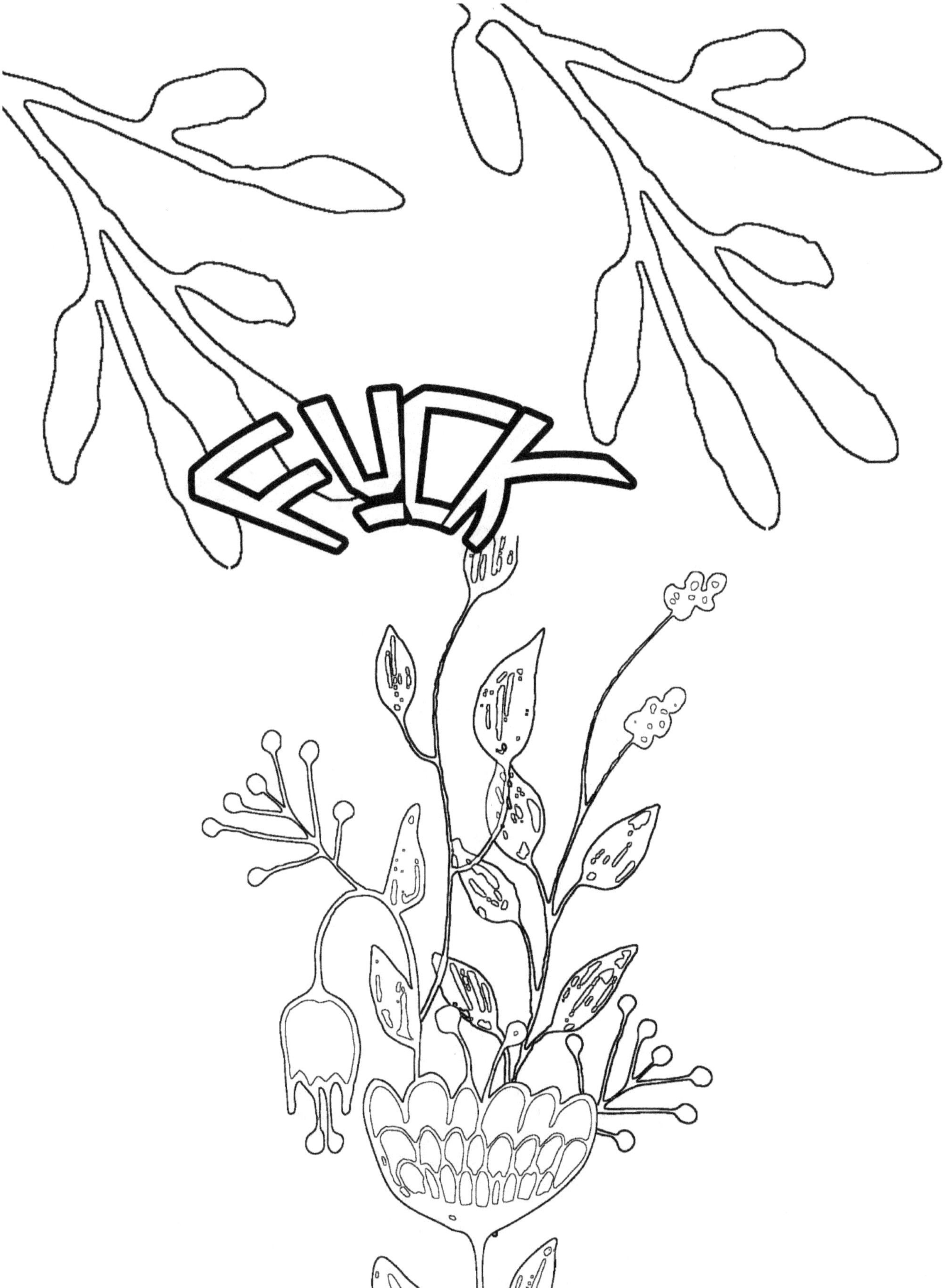
FUCK

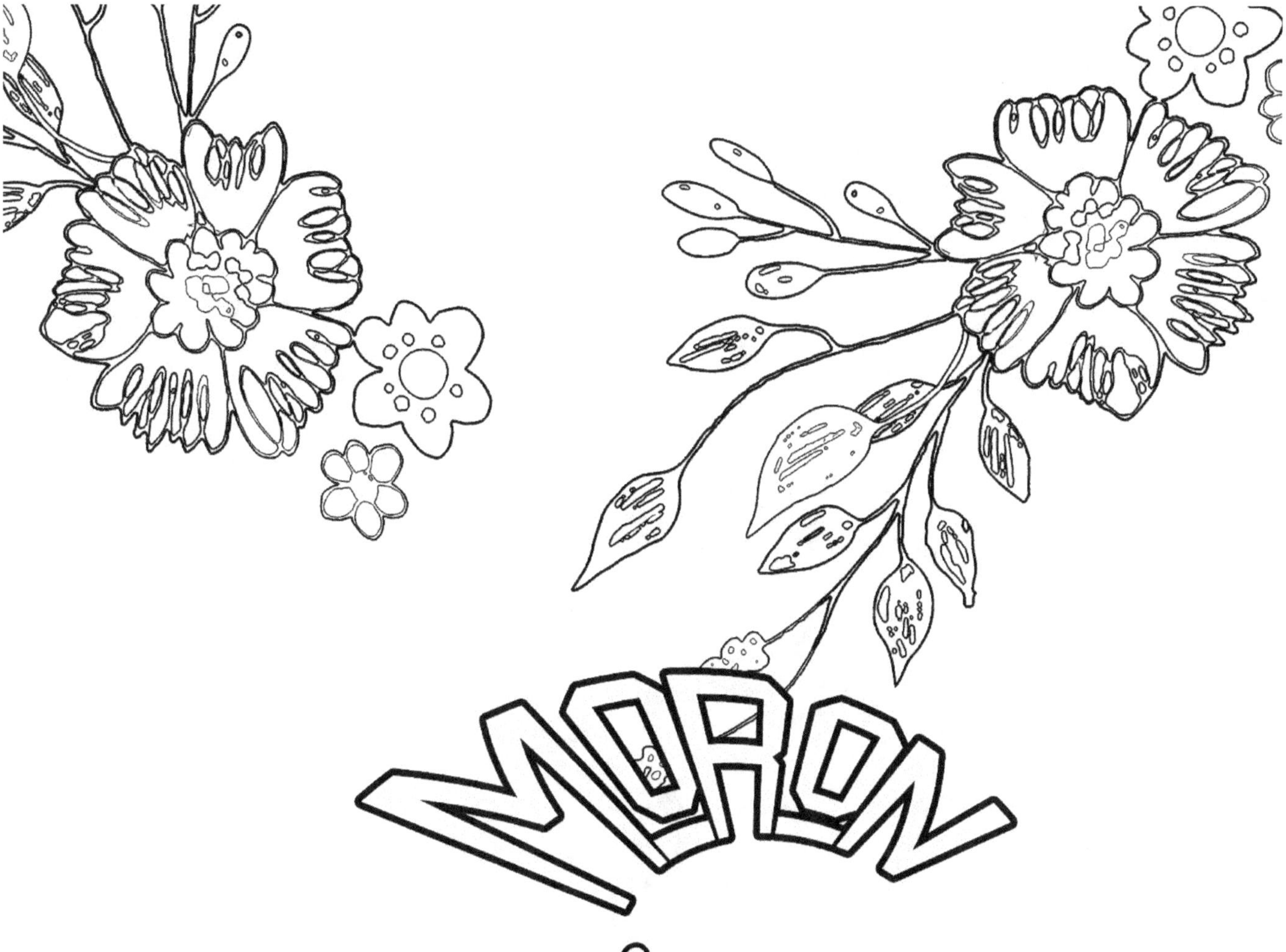
MORON

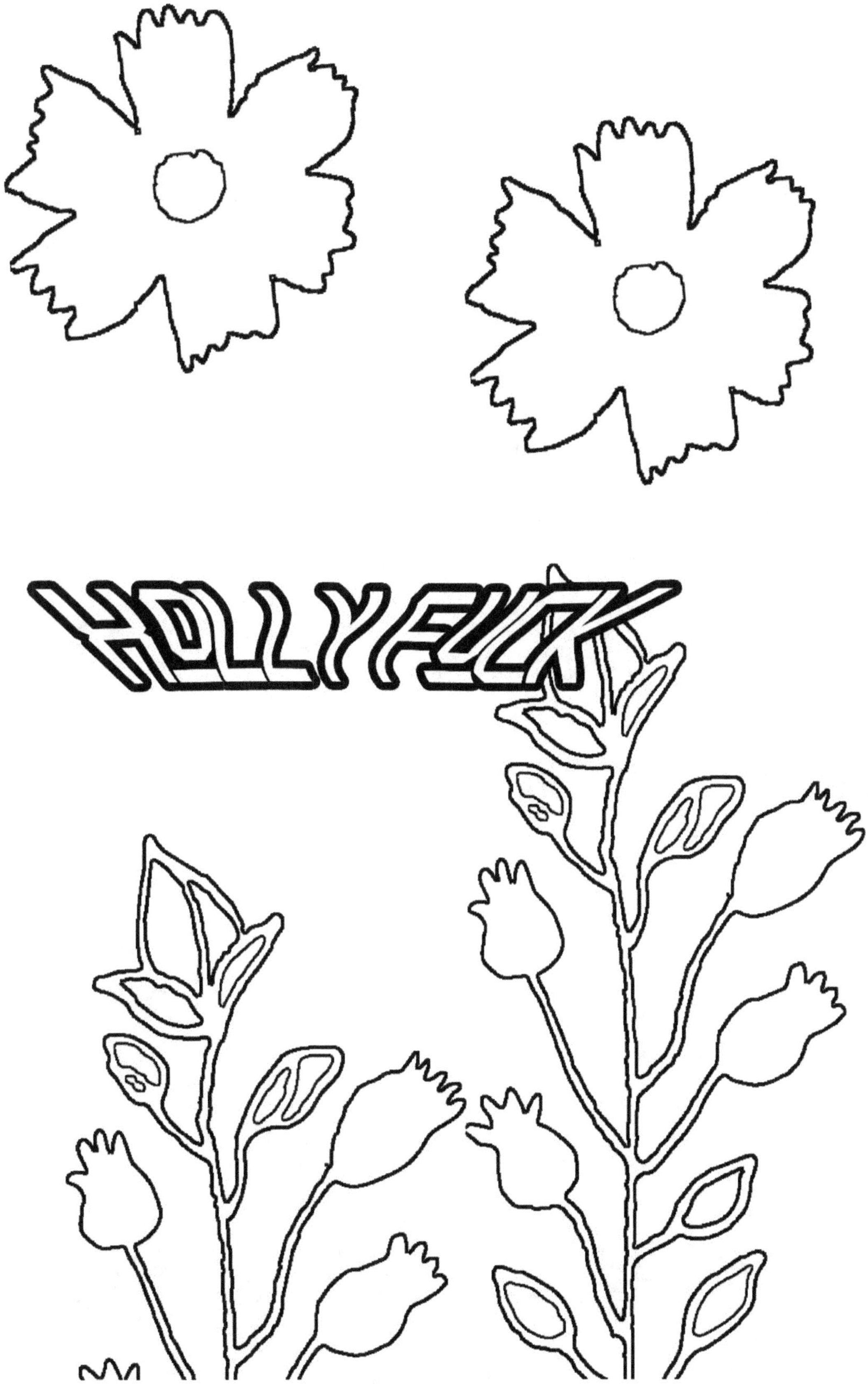
HOLLYFUCK

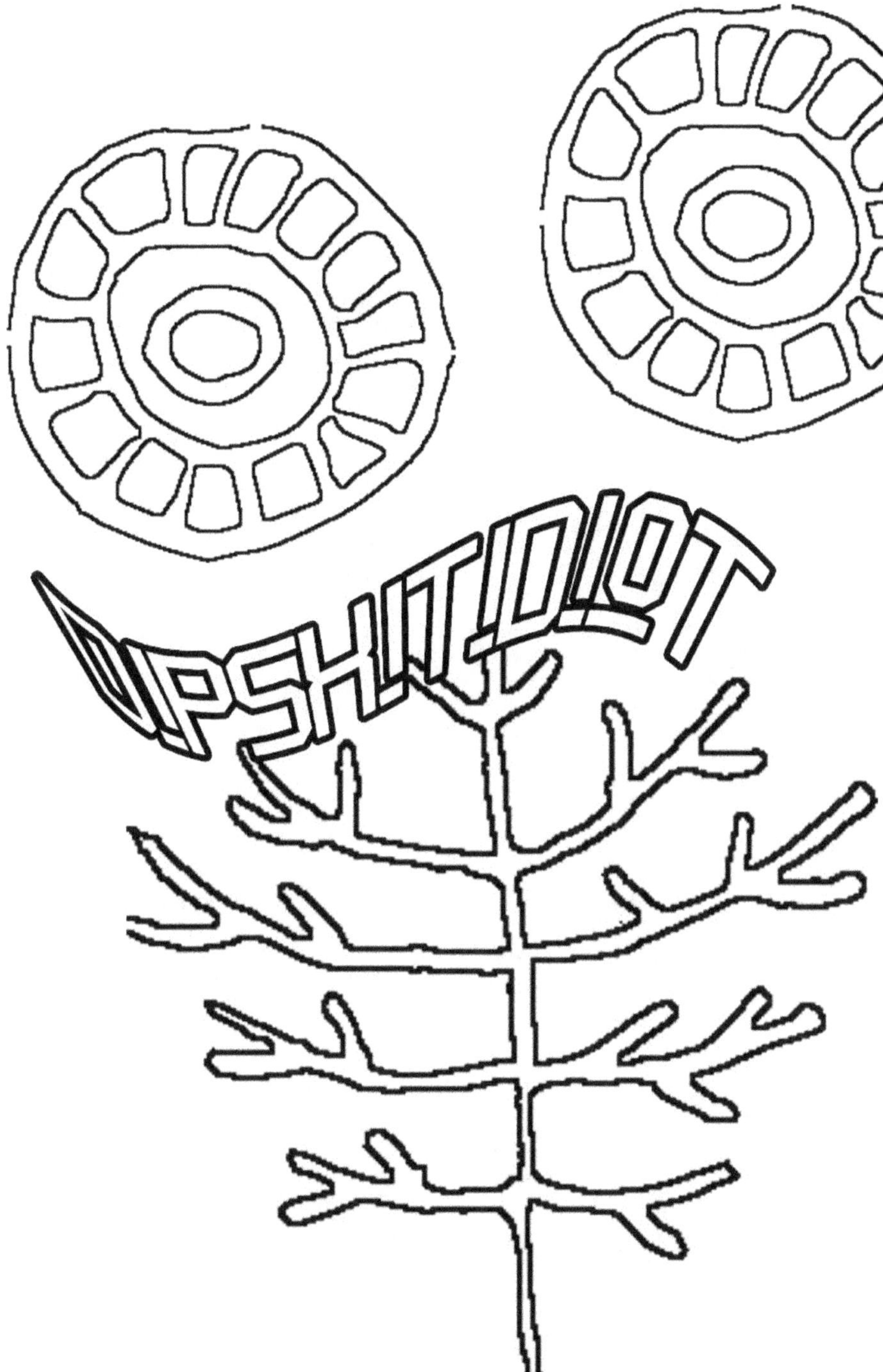
DIPSHITIDIOT

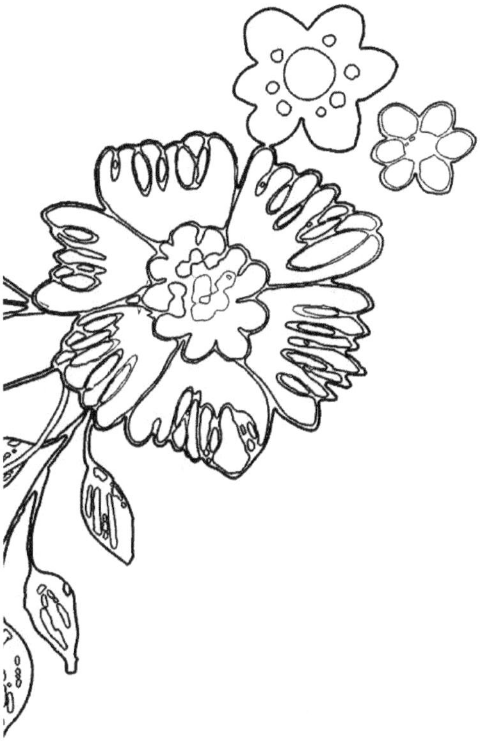

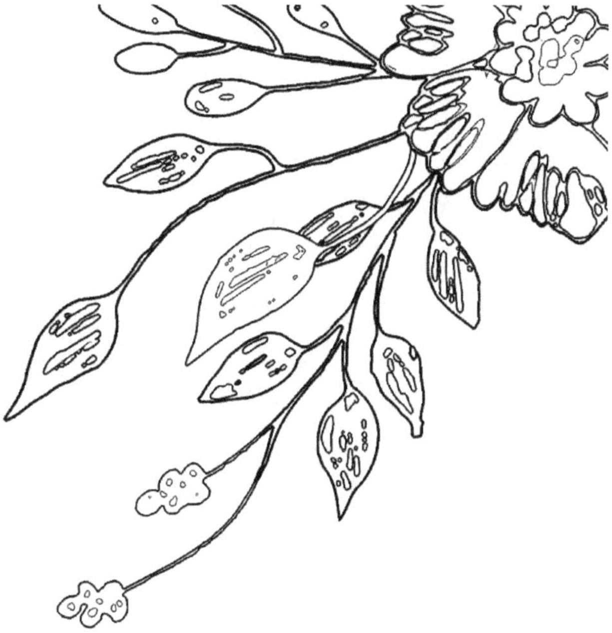

PISS OFF

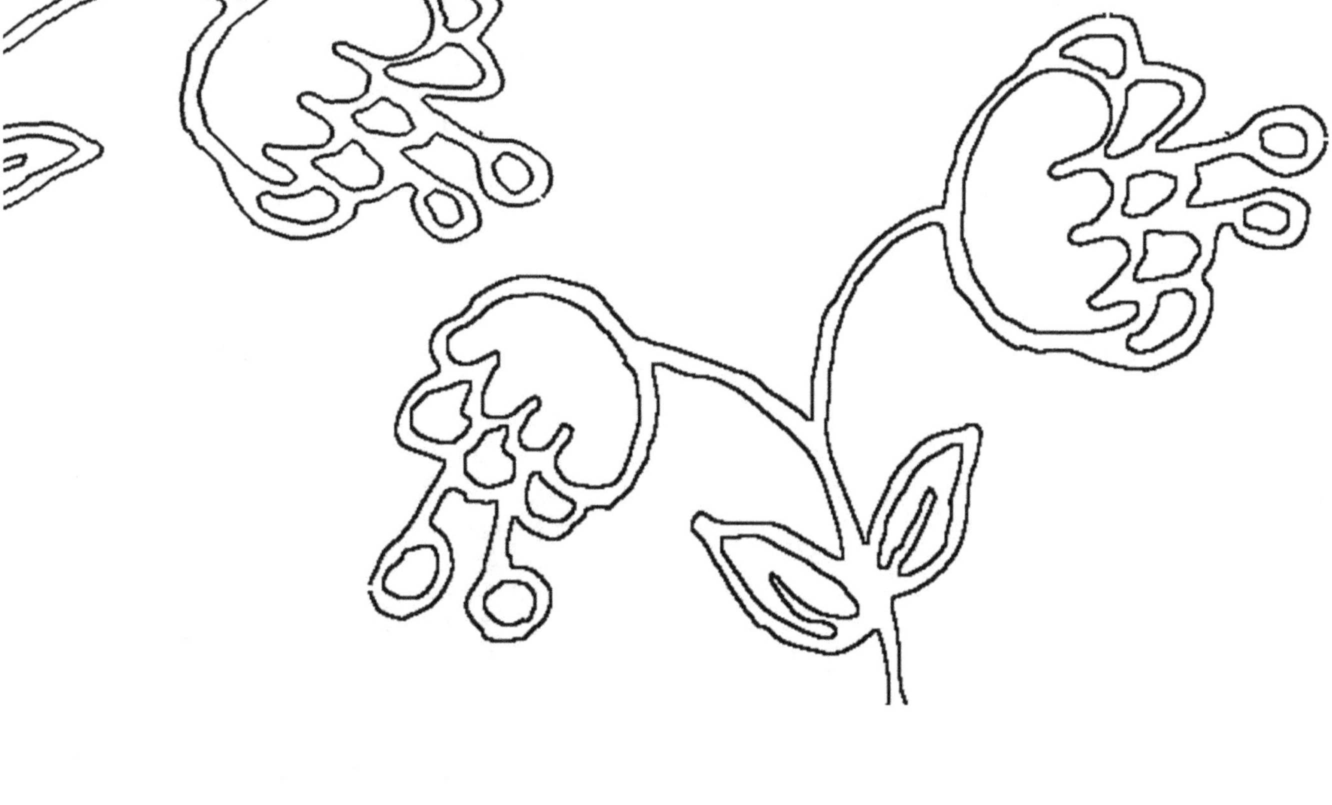

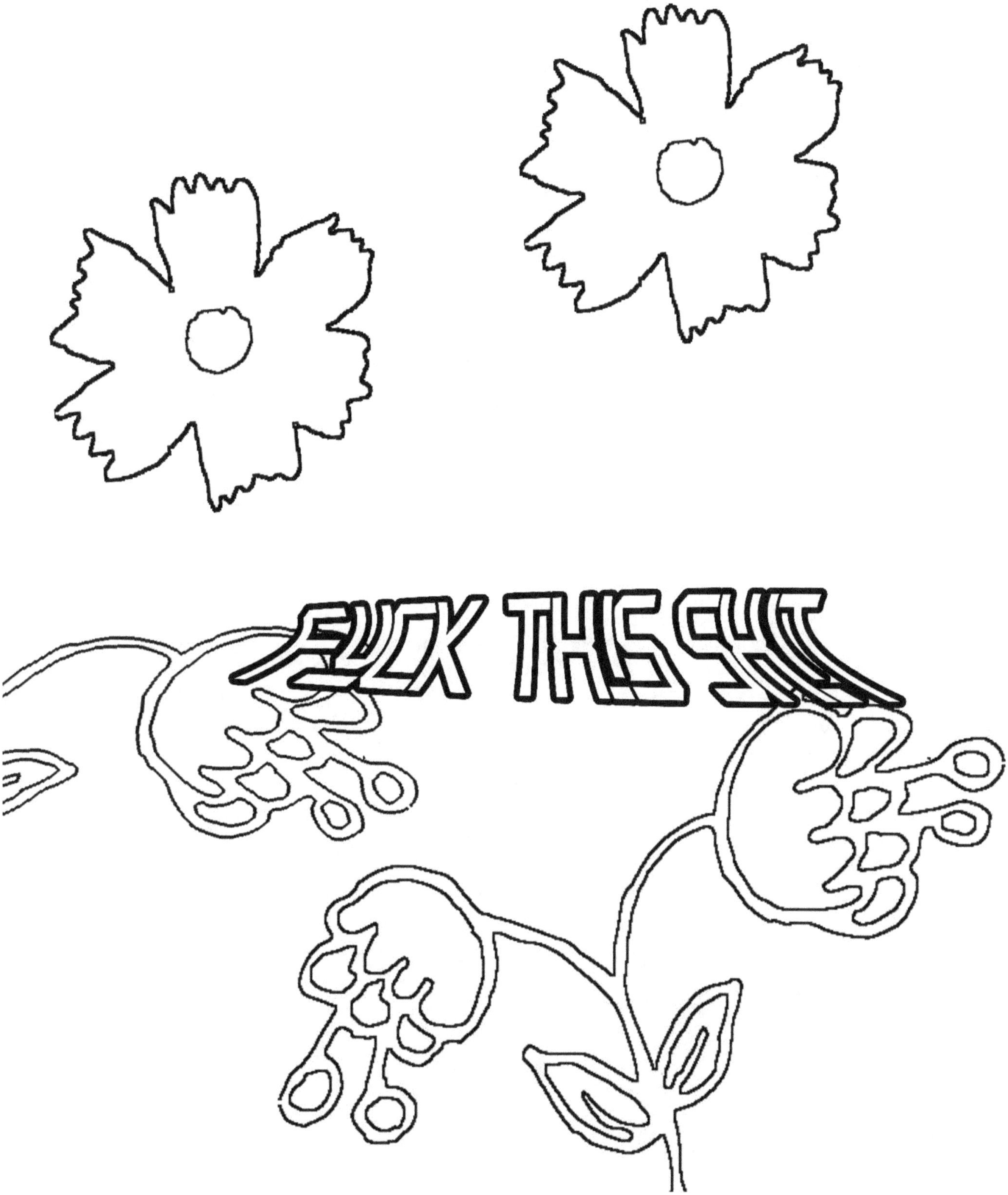
FUCK THIS SHIT

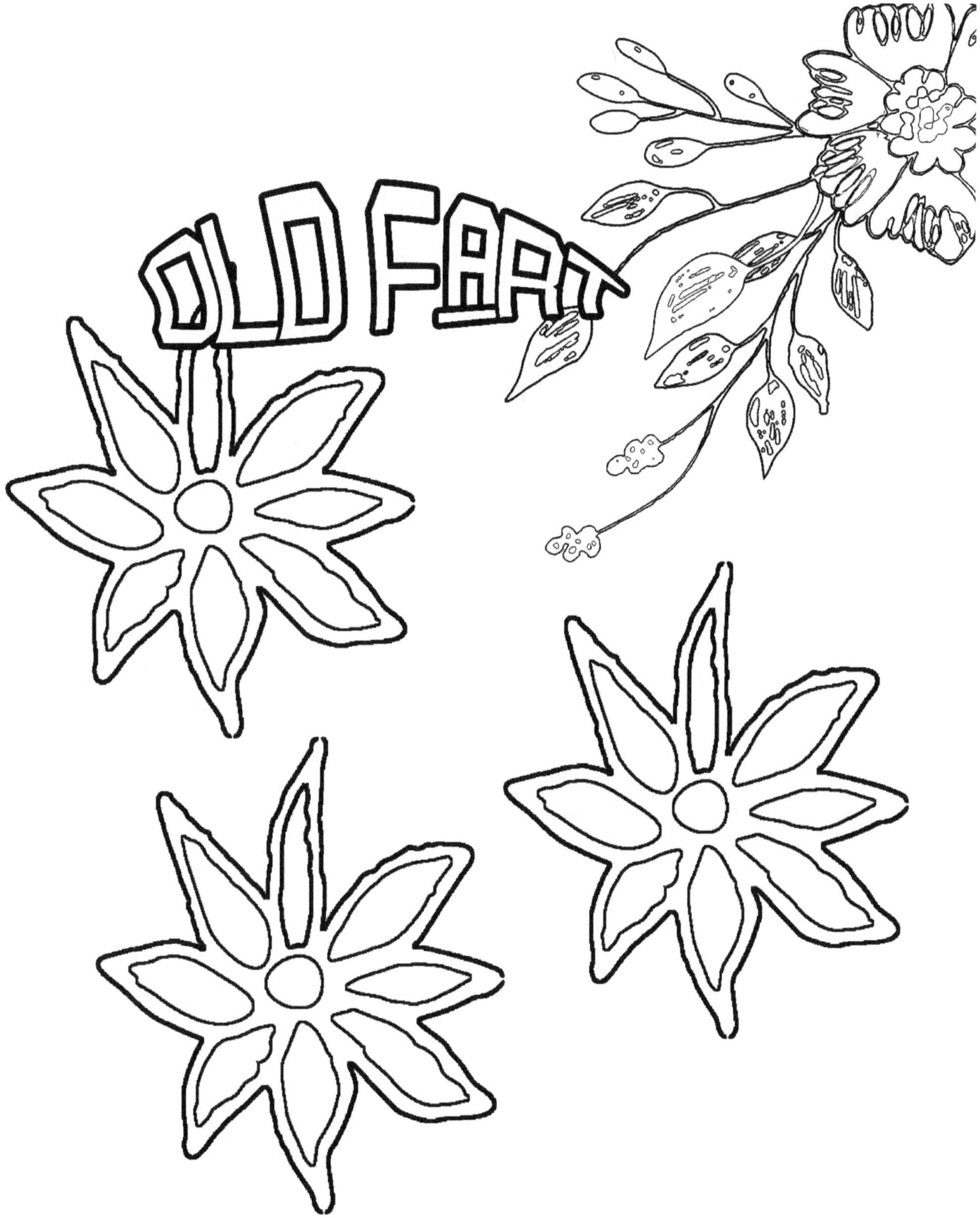
OLD FART

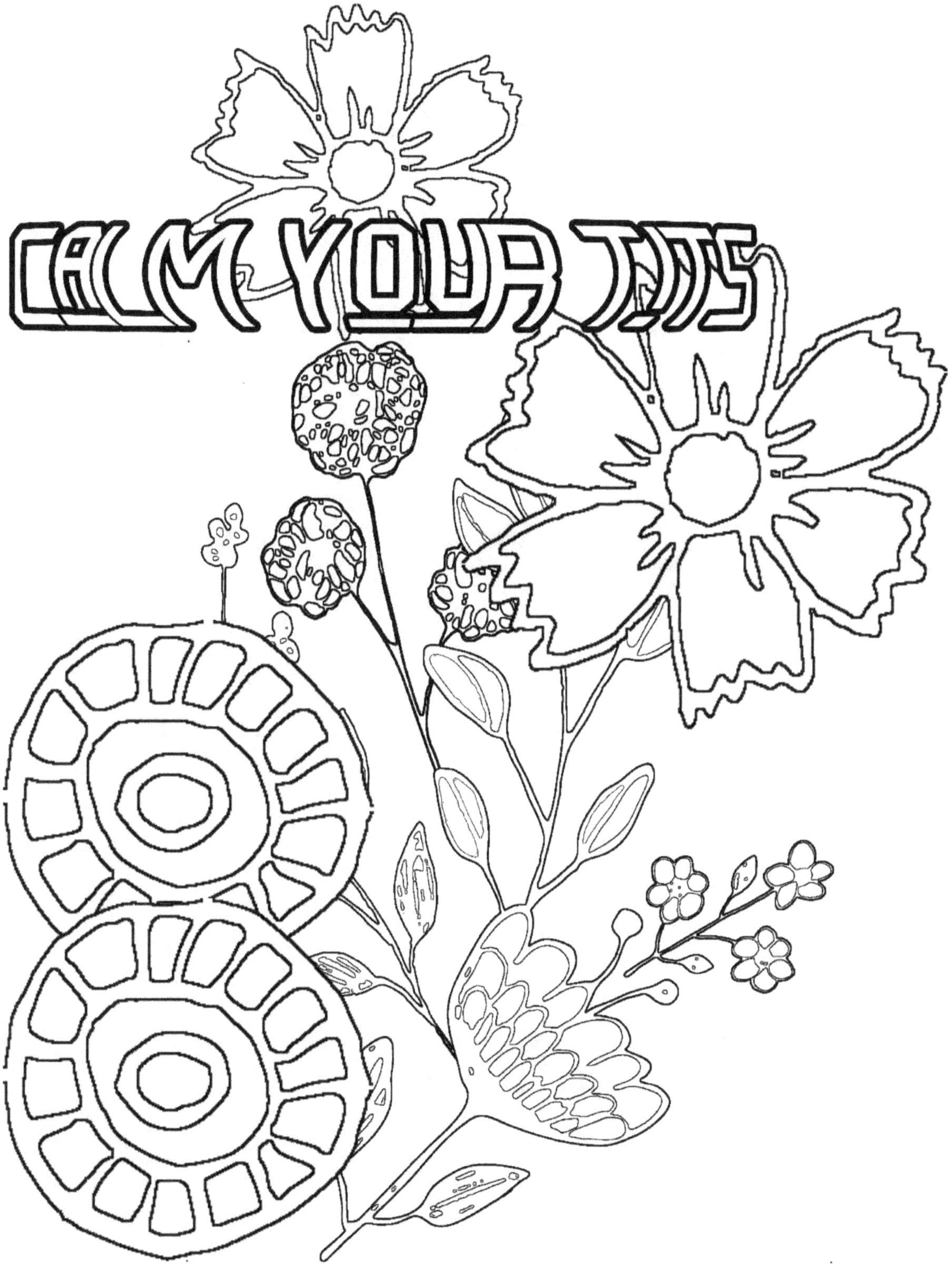
CALM YOUR TITS

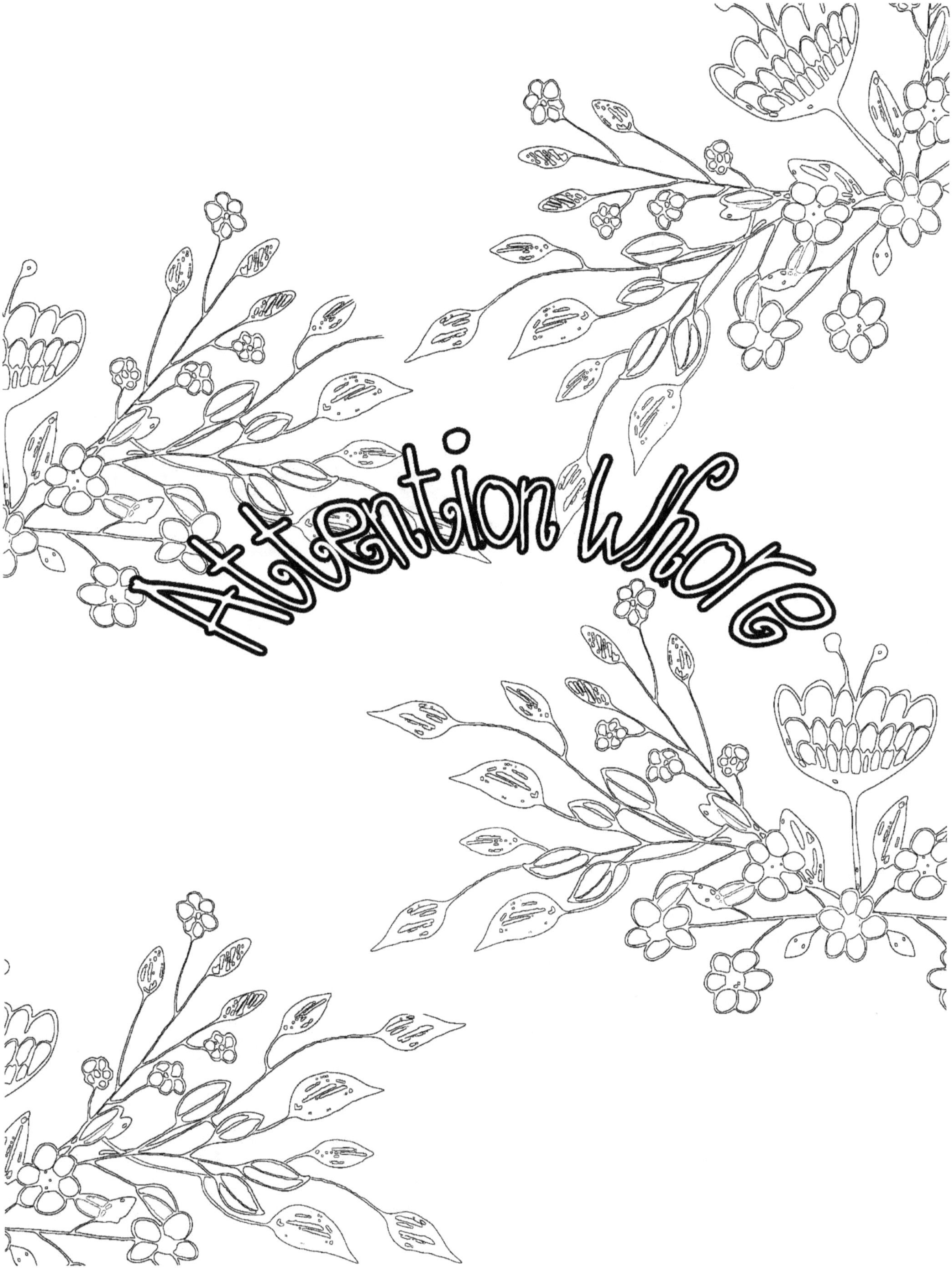
Attention Whore

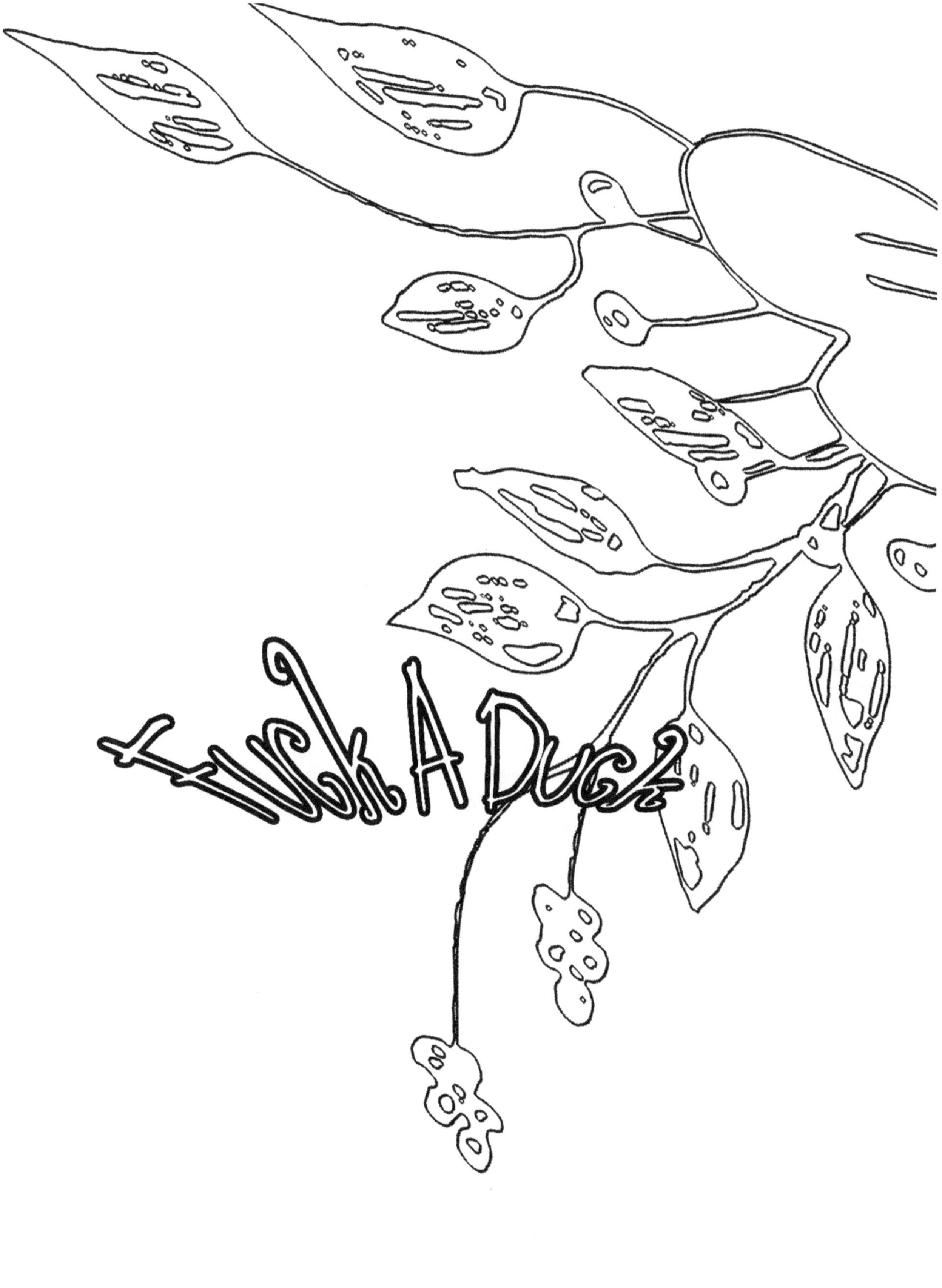
Fuck A Duck

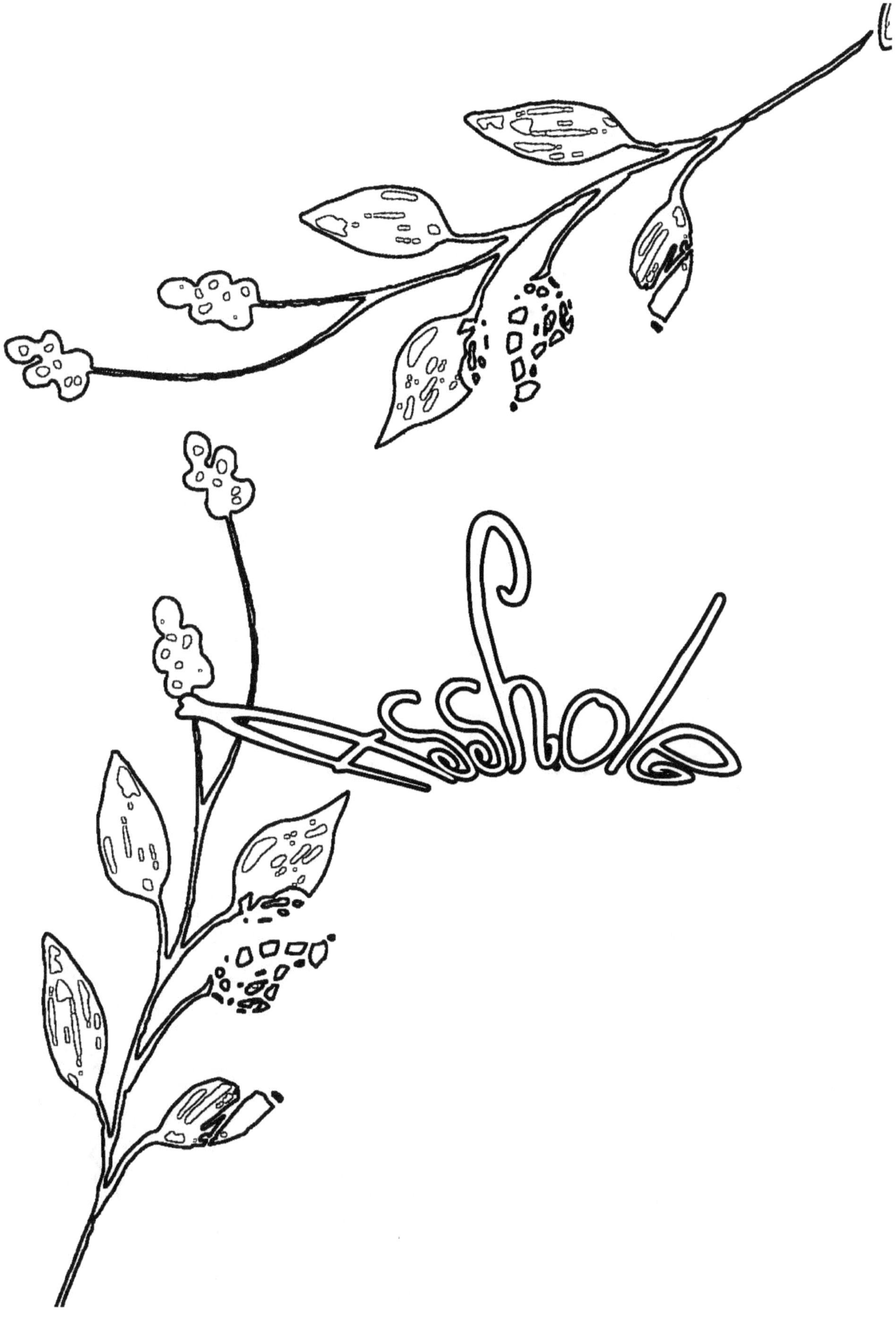
Asshole

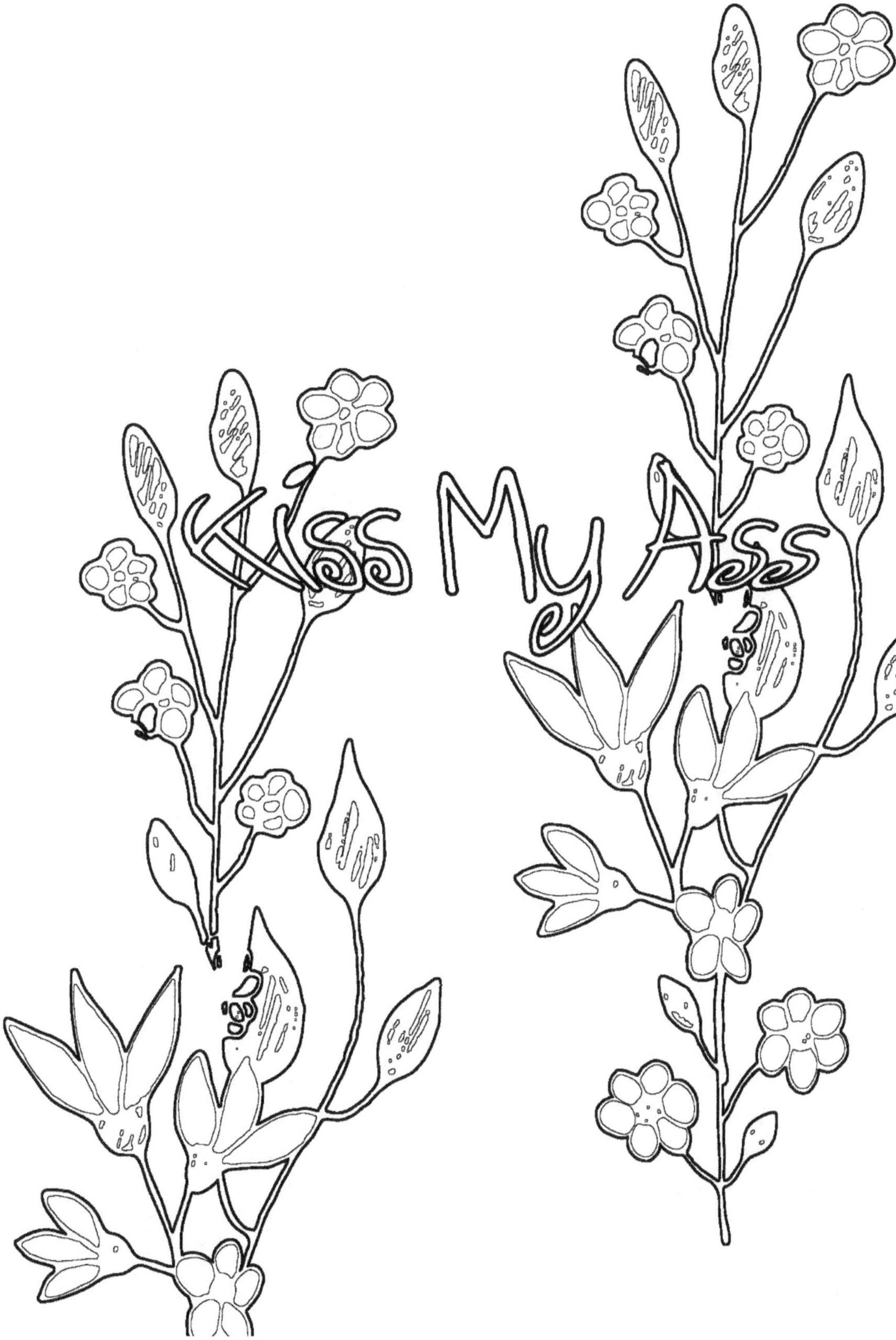
Kiss My Ass

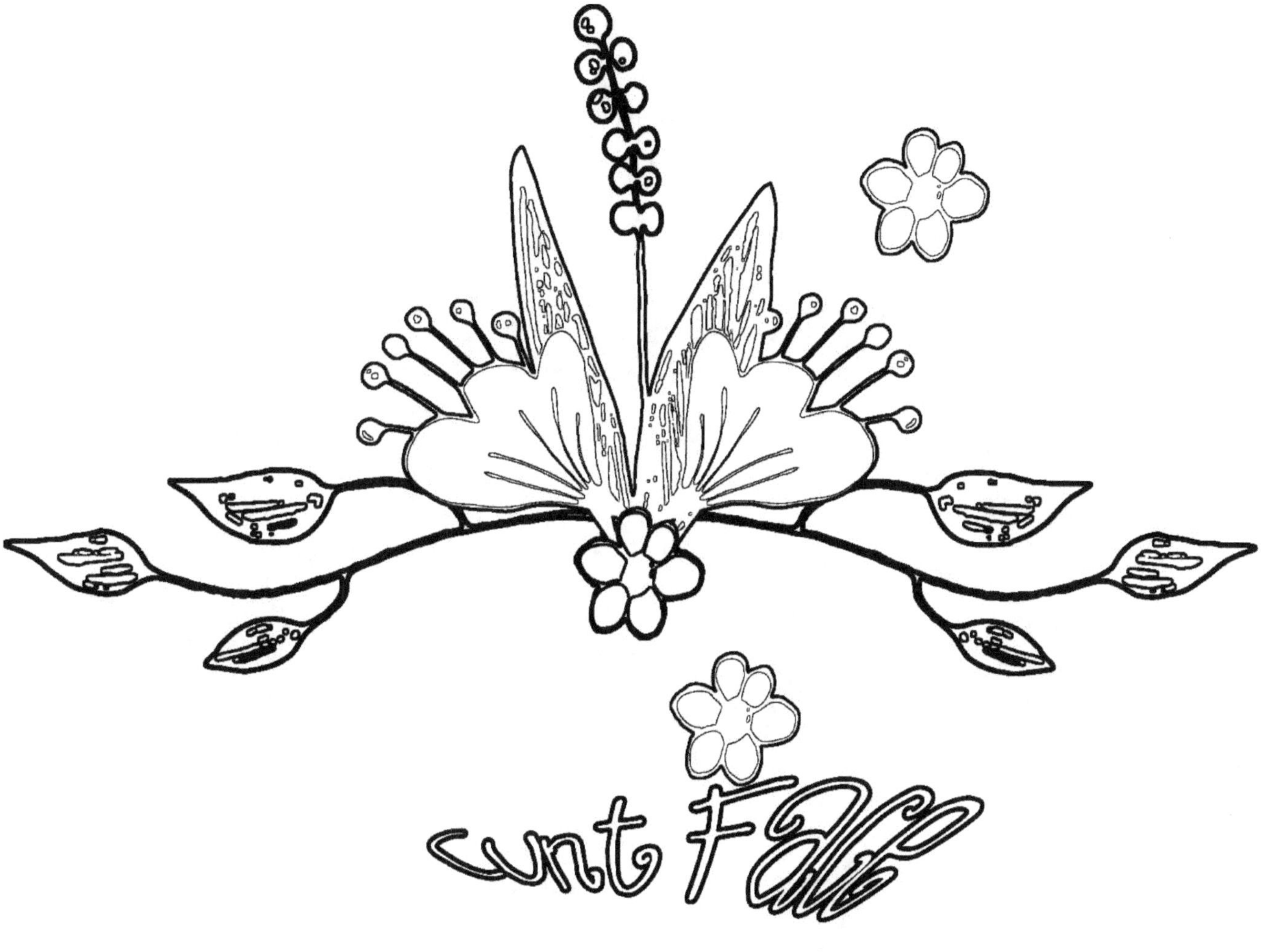
cunt

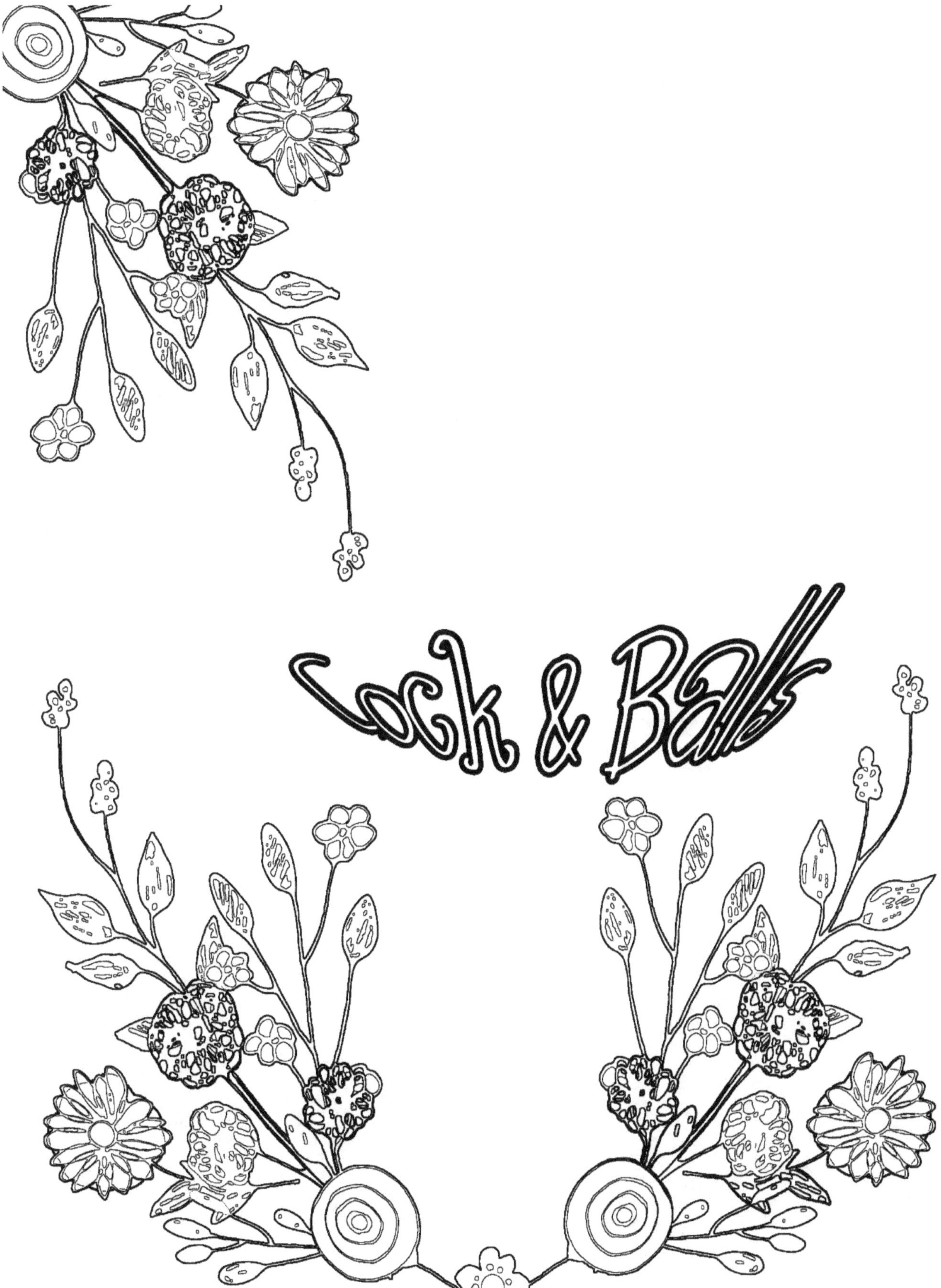
Cock & Balls

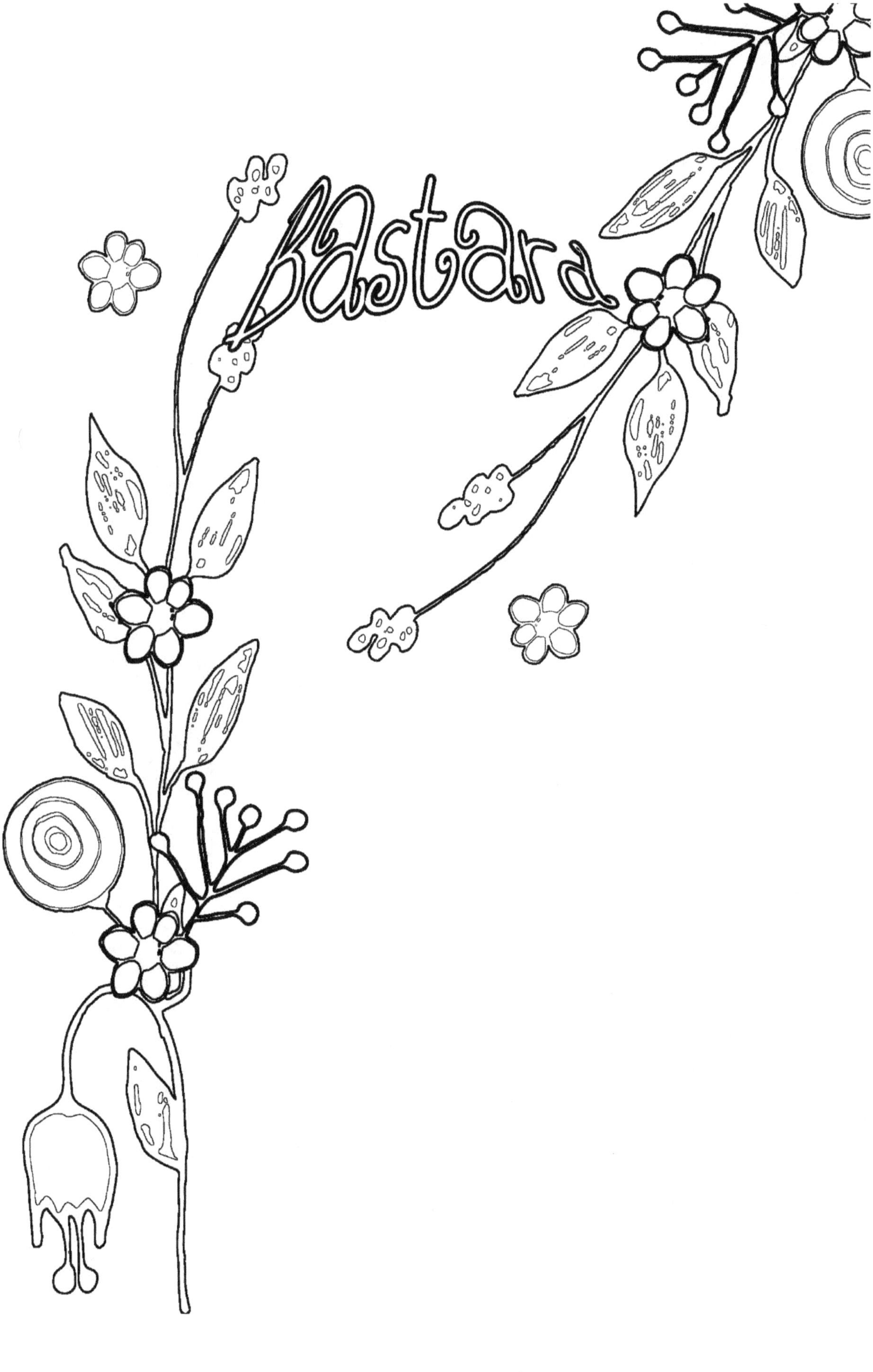
Bastarda

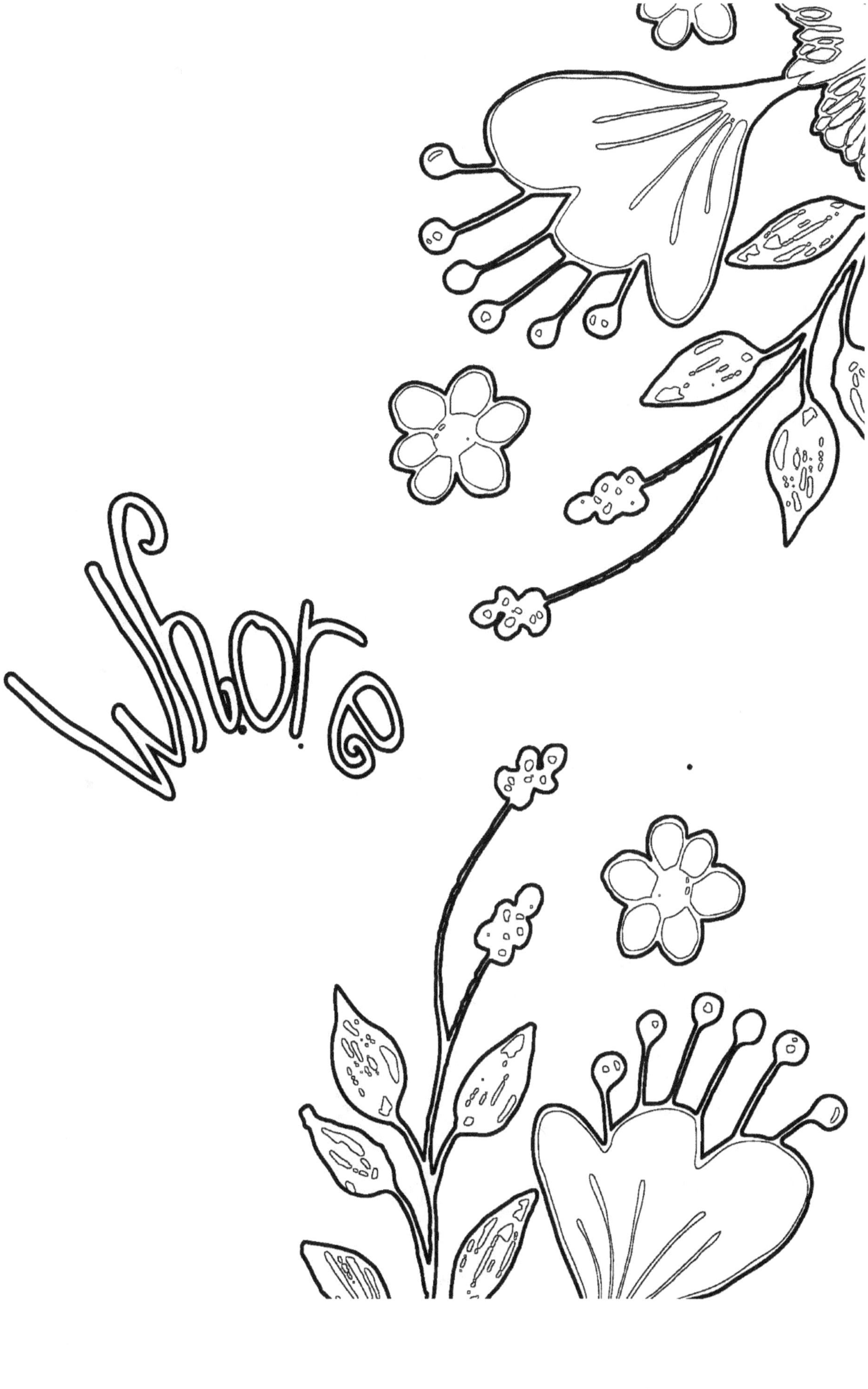
Whore

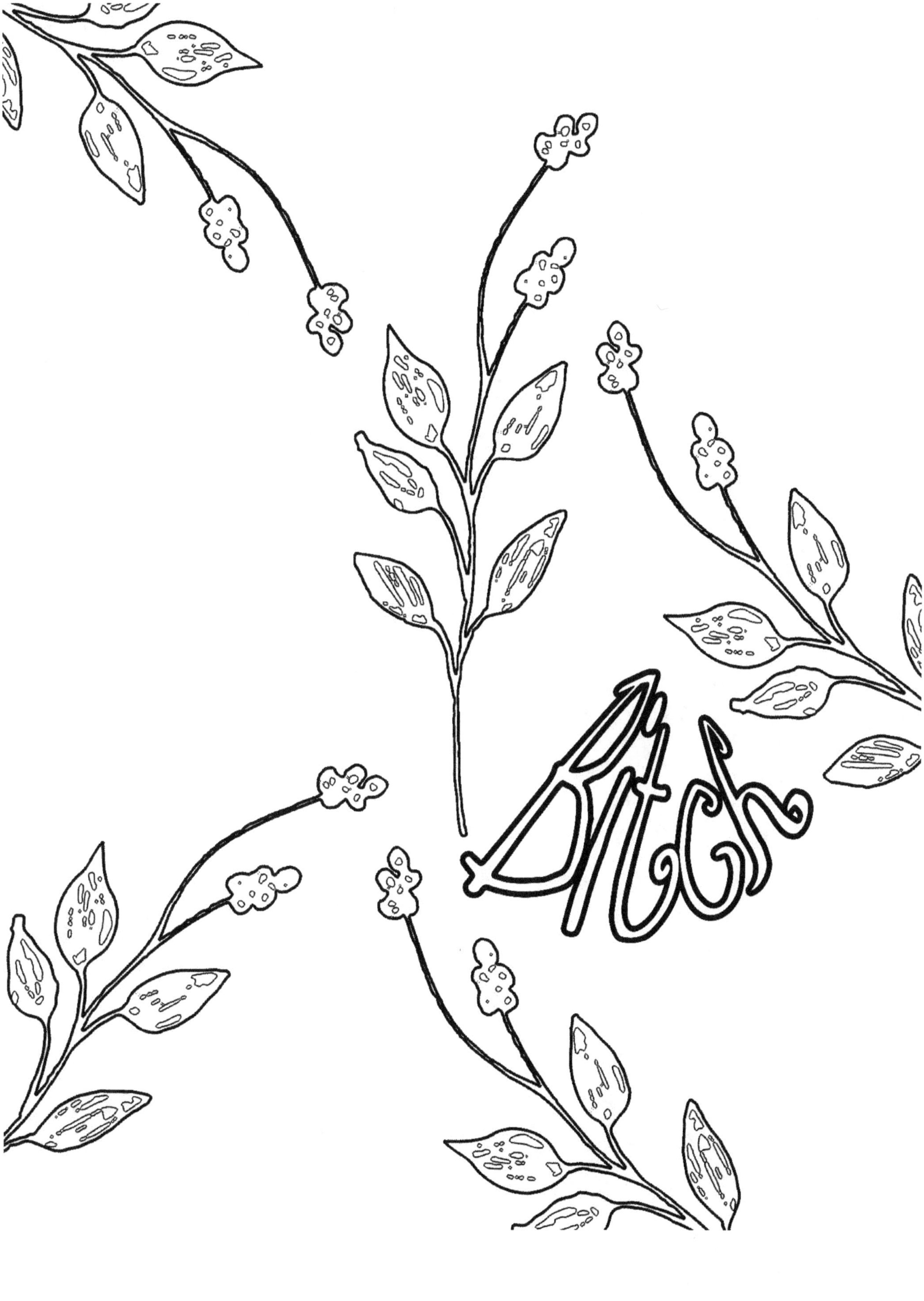
Bitch

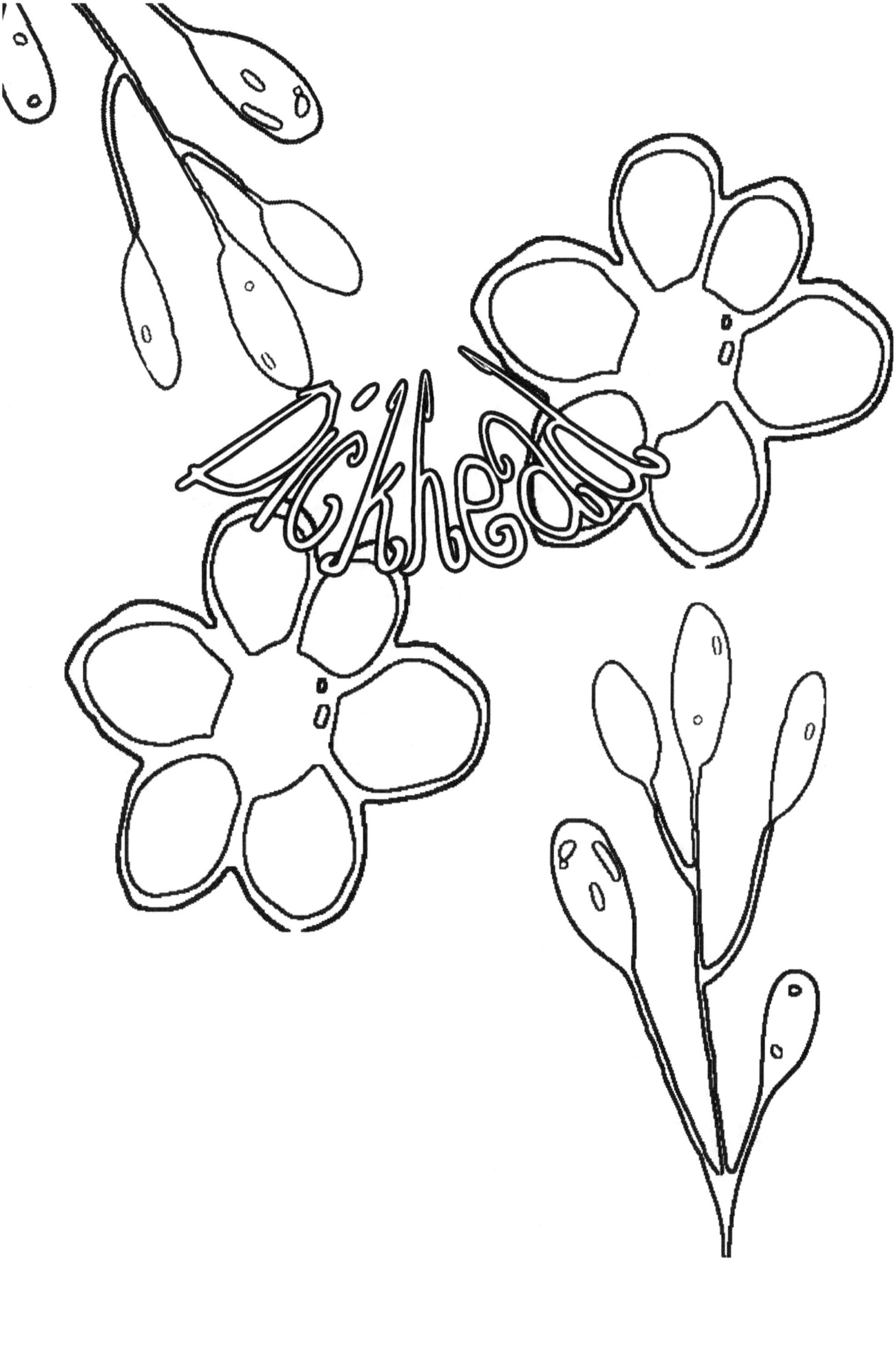
Dickhead

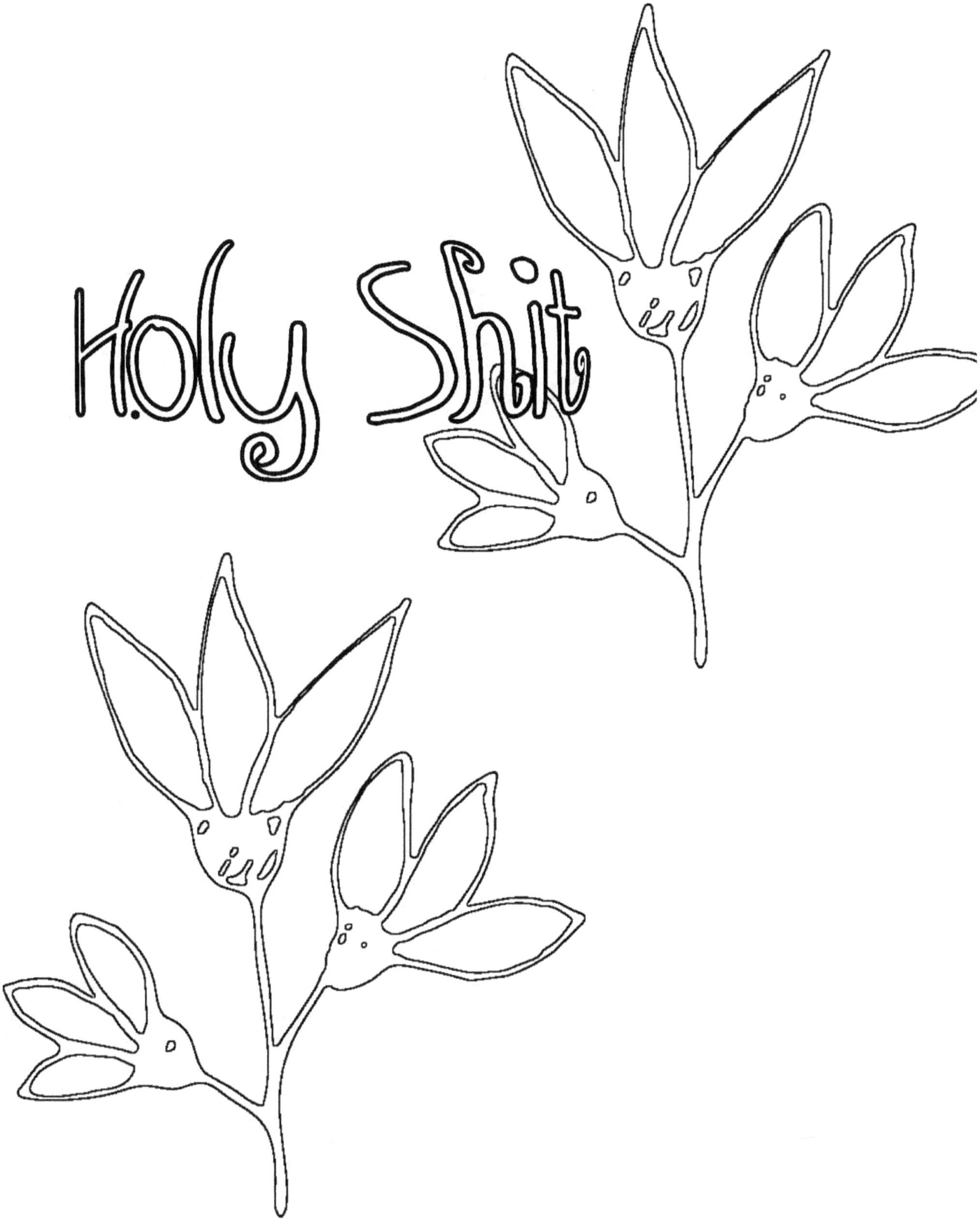
Holy Shit

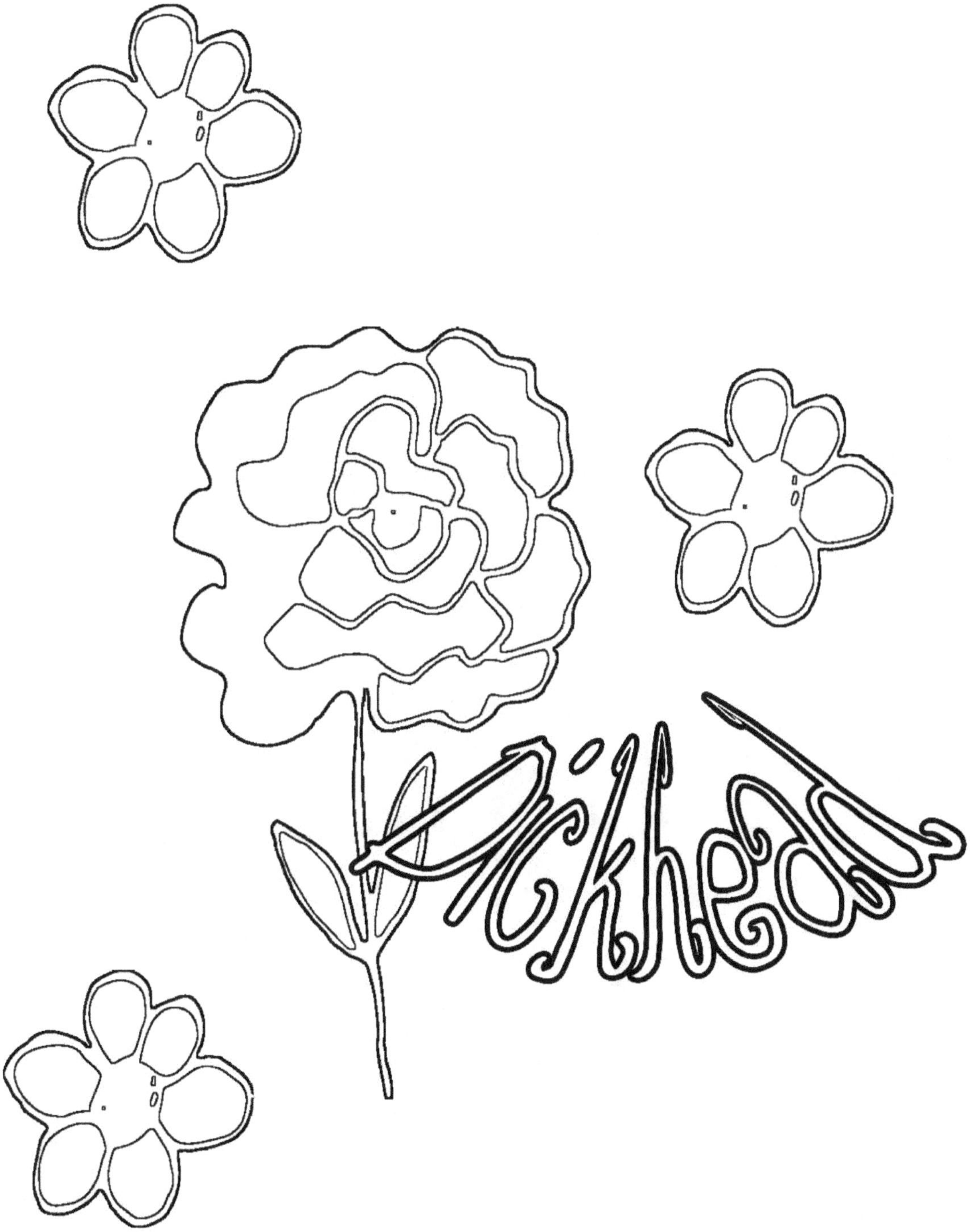
Dickhead

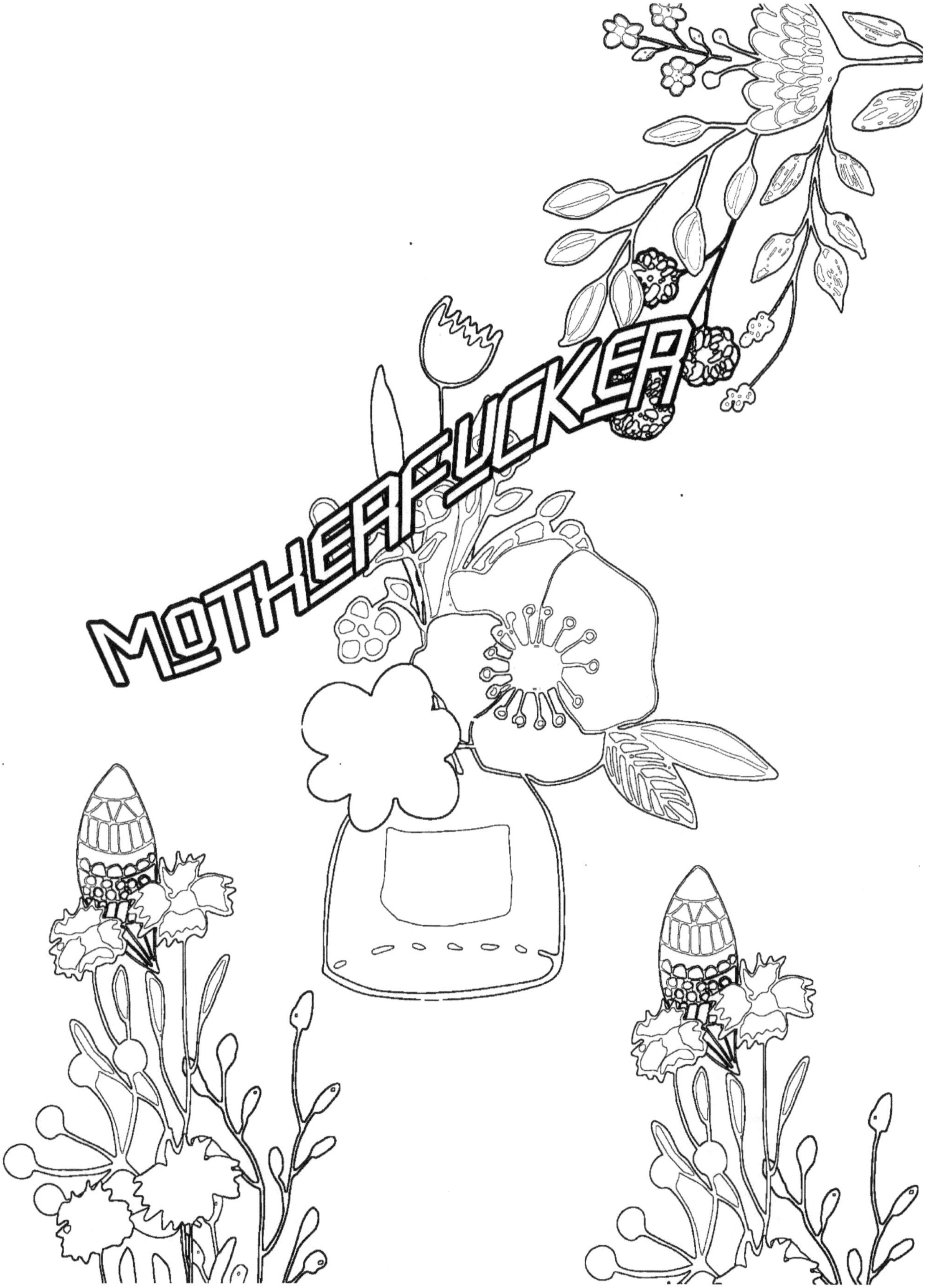
MOTHERFUCKER

www.ingramcontent.com/pod-product-compliance
Lightning Source LLC
Chambersburg PA
CBHW081749170526
45167CB00009B/3975
* 9 7 8 1 5 4 2 8 0 9 9 3 1 *